AF425936

Manifesting Dreams

Krysta Anderson

BookLeaf Publishing

Manifesting Dreams © 2023 Krysta Anderson

All rights reserved.

No part of this publication may be reproduced, stored in a retrieval system, or transmitted, in any form or by any means, electronic, mechanical, photocopying, recording or otherwise, without the prior written permission of the presenters.

Krysta Anderson asserts the moral right to be identified as author of this work.

Presentation by *BookLeaf Publishing*

Web: www.bookleafpub.com

E-mail: info@bookleafpub.com

ISBN: 9789357443074

First edition 2023

I hope that this book of poems will open your mind and take you on a journey that will change the way you look and feel about life by the end. The last few poems are a special treat so grab a cup of coffee or hot chocolate, settle in your favorite cozy spot, and enjoy the ride!!

ACKNOWLEDGEMENT

Thank you to the members of STARSET for being so amazing and down-to-earth, and for giving me the inspiration and courage to write my very first novel!

PREFACE

A world inspired by the band Starset. They are my all-time favorite band, because they have brought me to this magical world of exploration and wonder, and now I want to invite you to experience it as well! Most of the poems in here revolve around space, exploration, and looking out behind our world.

Choosing Dreams

Feeling so tired, but not being able to drift off...
Wanting to dream, but not sure of what.
No thoughts or wishes come to mind, but then..
I started wishing that I was in a land.
A land filled with peace and love.
But what exactly does that look like, I wonder?
A glistening waterfall flows down into a pond.
Butterflies flutter around happily, all sorts of
colors blending together as one.
Lush green trees great me as I walk towards the
waterfall.
The trees form a circle around me, almost as if
they could sense my presence.
A bed of lilies opens up towards the warmth of
the sun.
A flock of birds sing a tuneful song overhead,
Greeting the waterfall, with a fluorescent show.
I think to myself as I drift off to sleep,
This is where I want to be.
I'm happy, at peace and I feel free.
I never want to wake to the never-ending world.
The never-ending world of reality.

Where the Skies End

At the edge of the world
Fading into nothingness
Feel the darkness pulling you in
The moon goddess hides behind dark grey
clouds
As a black shadow looms in the wind
Ocean waves beat against the shore
A lasting reminder of what once was, is no more
Where the skies end
Is where I'll stay
Stuck in between night and day
Feeling the pull of the waves drag me away
Fading into nothingness
My dreams a lasting reminder of where I've
been
At the edge of the world is where I remain
Where the skies end is my domain

Gravity

Splish splash, soak relax
Dip your toes in the turquoise waters
Discovering a gem in the night like a little
Knick-knack
The coolness of the water sends a little shiver up
your spine
Walking until you're in waist-deep, take a deep
breath
And let out a sigh of relief
As the sun dips below the horizon
Strings of lights come to life, illuminating the
night in a warm glow
Looking up at the stars in disbelief
You see the moon smiling as it emanates like
Calypso
Underneath a sky full of stars
All sorts of colors that twinkle and shine
Riding the horizon is where the moon will rise
My heart unveiling
In the gravity of the moon

Gorgeous Nightmare

A beautiful dream turns into a gorgeous
nightmare
You're never going to beat it
You gotta stop pretending
But someday you're gunna wake up
And realize that you're life has been sending
Messages like a calling
Dreams become reality, and you feel like you're
falling

Into the abyss of the unknown
A sweet lullaby plays through your mind
A calling from deep inside your heart
Telling you that you've grown
A dark shadow looms over your shoulder
The feeling of dread soon taking over

Wanting to push forward, but not knowing how
Sweat beads up on your forehead
As you furrow your brow
Not knowing which way to turn
A hopeful feeling soon coming to fruition
You make a turn towards the anticipated
acquisition

A beautiful dream turns into a gorgeous
nightmare
But this time around, you know how to
overcome that affair

Haiku Times Two

Manifest your dreams
Random, weird, or not
Turn your wishes into a reality

~~~~~ ~~~~~ ~~~~~ ~~~~~ ~~~~~ ~~~~~

A wish made on a falling star:
A hope made on a dandelion
A dream cast towards the moon
~~~~~

Good & Evil

His eyes were a soft blue.
His hair silky black.
His skin tone fair and even,
He was an angel sent from above.
Godsend and handsome,
He was the chosen one.

Her hair was a light blonde.
Her eyes sparkled a deep hazel hue.
Her skin tone was tan and soft,
She was a demon born to life.
Beautiful and seductive,
She was the chosen star.

They had met on a rainy night.
On a city street they each flew.
Searching for the same thing.
She had arrived first,
But his presence won her over.
Together a bond was connected.
Good and Evil.
Darkness and Light.
Together, they shared the world.

Memories

Even though time has passed by,
I still cry .
I still feel the same way I did that day,
When I said my last goodbye.
Never did I want that day to come,
For you were my best friend.
The rock that held me through every storm.
You were the shield in my battles,
Giving me strength and endurance through my
hard times.
I told everything to you,
Because I knew you went through the same
things before.
I still remember the day I graduated
kindergarten,
You were there by my side.
You gave me words of guidance and peace,
When my heart needed it the most.
You gave me love when I thought I had nowhere
to go.
Your words and memories are what keep me
going.
Your everlasting flowery scent and your
beautiful eyes stay in my memories.

They wash over me as if it were just yesterday
that I was last with you.
Your love healed me and made me stronger.
You taught me that there is a Heaven,
And I believe that that's where you are. Our true
home.
I will never forget you my sweet Great
Grandmother.
And I know we'll be together again someday,
with Him.
Never shall we be apart,
For you will always be in my heart.

In loving memory of my Great Grandmother
who passed away from Pancreatic Cancer~April
15th, 2014~

Freedom

His eyes stare into mine,
Dark blue with specks of grey.
Warmth and longing course through us as we
stand on a cliff, finally free.
Stepping out of a burning world,
With ashes that swirled.
Filling the skies and sticking to our
sweat-barren skin.

Together we ran into the forest,
Running wild and free.
Together we set out to create a new world.
One without war and fear.
We wanted to start a new world,
Where we could cheer.
We would be the loudest of all people.
Letting our voices cry out, as we were free.

Forgetting all those who wasted their time in a
steeple.
We wanted to be free.
And now we finally were.
Together we ran into the forest.
Laughing heartily, holding hands.
Living out our fantasy, freer than we could ever
be.

Away We Go Now

Into the unknown
How far will we go?
Based on what we know
What is high and what is low?
Away we go now, to the stars

We reach out far
Our hands outstretched towards the sky
Wishing we all had wings
So we could fly
Like Icarus going into the sun
We run like the wind
And aim like a loaded gun
Into the unknown we go
Searching for a new world
That can stun like the sun

Lift off and away we go
Leaving the world behind
Waving to people we pass by
As they shovel the snow
Feeling the warmth of the stars
We don't need to worry about breathing here
For we belong amongst the stars
Leaving this world behind with no fears
Away we go now

Siren's Echo

There's no room for fairytales here
A burgundy red ship sails on rough seas
Dark cloudy skies bring a warning that
something gloomy is near
Entering through high-strung hills and cliffs
There is no room for uncertainty here

As the sailors prepare for what lies ahead
The light ocean waters turn into a milky white
Bits of rocks bounce off of the ships' bow
A sight lay out before the sailors, etched into
history now
A graveyard of ships from every era
Lines the shoreline on both the starboard and
port side

Nervousness settles in each sailor's stomach
Which were not full
Something stirred in the murky waters
A melodic sound filled their ears and echoed off
of the ships' hull
A blue shimmering fin tails causes a splash
And as the siren emerged from the water

Her striking long blonde hair accentuated her
sleek curves
She smiled then, and began to sing her tune
But the sailors noticed something peculiar about
the sound
Something called each of their names
Pulling at their heartstrings, like a burning flame
Hearing the echo call to broken hearts
The siren took over the crew, tearing their minds
apart

Soaring

Into the skies we go
Far above, not below
Into the universe
Floating around in the unknown
Past the moon, far beyond
Distant stars, the ones that we know
Go ahead and outstretch your hands

Into the sky we go
Not sure yet where to roam
The universe moving so fast
So many different directions to go
All things back on Earth, now in the past
Go ahead and lose your fears
Show me the smile that I love, as I wipe away
your tears

Go ahead and stretch out your hand, my dear
Let your fears go
And let yourself drift off to where we are, here
Imagine yourself as if your toes are in the sand
Floating in between the stars
Look at the distance we are from Earth
Watch in amazement as a star lands in your hand
Into the unknown we go
Soaring through the stars that glow

Becoming You

Take your pain and wash it away
Let the past flow from your grasp
As the warm water cleans your wounds
The soothing sensation like time in the sand
dunes

Take a step outside and look up at the sky
Feel the coolness of the air
Kissing your cheeks and playing in your hair
Watch in awe as a comet soars by
Through the night sky

Take a deep breath
Close your eyes
And let it out slowly
Feel your soul connecting with the universe
As the moon shows its smile
Brightening the sky, but still allowing the stars
to shine

Open your eyes and see the world
Sure, it might be far from perfect
But if you take a step back
And take a different look at it
You'll be sure to see

The world and the galaxy
And like an oyster you found in the sea
Holding in your hand, the pearl
For the world to see

Leaving the Past, there

Pretty consistent on a futuristic line
The world seeming so far away
You can't see it's shine
The world aglow from the stars above
There's nothing to be gained
From roaming alone

Imagine a star landing in your hand
Warm to the touch
And on its own, it stands
Pulsing like a heart beats
The star hums a beautiful sound
Grasping you in its clutch

The pureness of the heart
Makes others want to take advantage
But don't let that stop you
From seeing the advantage
From a different point of view

If you are kind to all souls
Then something may come to be
The stars in the sky
Are aligning for you tonight
Your heart opens up

Feeling love and acceptance entering your soul
Your heart wanting to fly, as if it were a
hummingbird
Ready to fly free

Views

Guide me down to the world below
Plant my feet in the snow
Show me what there is to see
Help set me free

Seeing the world from above
Floating through and in between the novas
Giving the rope around your waist a tug
Back to the ship, you float
The ship known as the Vista

Named after a gorgeous mountain top from back
home
The spaceship holds a warm glow
After you enter and get changed
You take a seat at the helm, waiting to see the
range apart from the unknown below

Watch in content as the stars and fellow galaxies
wave hello
A smile lights up your features, then
As you wonder
How far can we go?

Forever Together

Young and beautiful.
Youthful and free.
Souls bound together,
Forever together they would be.

She lie next to him,
Blissfully happy and madly in love.
He had his arms wrapped protectively around
her,
Whispering to her that he would never let go.
She stroked his muscled arm,
Warm to the touch and smooth as silk.
He rest his chin atop her head, his free hand
stroking her hair.

Together they could overpower anything.
Together they could become king and queen, in
their own world that is.
But most importantly,
Together they would forever be free.

Young and beautiful.
Youthful and free.
Souls bound together.
Forever together they would be.

In the Forest

In the forest we lay.
Side by side.
Hand in hand.
Together happy and un-afraid.
The trees stir softly with the breeze
Bringing out a sweet scent of calm.
The birds sing a tuneful song,
Ever so graceful and at peace.
The world seemed to spin around us
As we lie in the forest, breathing in Mother
Nature with every breath.

Being apart, the world seemed cold.
Empty streets and desolate places.
Facaded buildings and rundown signs.
No one to run to, for no one was there.
But together, we powered through.
I was with him wherever he went and he did the
same for me.
At the end of the day, all that mattered was that
we were together.

In the forest we lay.
Side by side.
Hand in hand.

Together happy and un-afraid.
Together, we would be.

22

Winter Prince

Black feathers flutter around
In a fury of darkness and cold wind
They form into the Winter Prince
Hand clenched on his sword that's strapped to
his side
The Winter Prince goes to see the King

People stay out of his way
For rumor goes around even to this day
Saying that the Winter Prince
And his sour mood has come again

But nobody knows who he truly is
For the Winter Prince in his wake, is never
moody, nor ever sour
When his season comes around
He's at his brightest and most at ease
The Winter Prince strides past the people
Like a rolling wave from the seas

Some people can't seem to look away from him
For he carries himself like a handsome
gentleman
Hair as black and soft as silk
Contrasts against his pale smooth skin

His clothes are that of a deep frosty blue
And no sky can compare to his icy blue eyes

Striding into the palace
The Winter Prince lets himself get anxious
In hopes that his King has good news
Hoping that the gates to their city are free
No fear can stop the Winter Prince
From serving his people
To the very end of his days

Spring Prince

As the flowers come into full bloom
The Spring Prince brings new life and new hope
Replenishing the land after the Winter Prince
Has passed on his Season
Guarding the city with his life

The Spring Prince never feels anything but joy
And happiness when he's on his way
To see the King of the Seasons
Curious as to what he has to say

As he rides on his chocolate colored steed
Through the fields of flowers
Where the children laugh and play
As he passes them by, they giggle and say 'hi'
Knowing that he and his brothers
Do a good job when guarding the city

Colorful hair sporting colors of different
Shades and hues
Colors like purple, green, yellow, and pink
And eyes that seem to glow like open blue skies
With robes that fit him perfectly
Vibrant colors of greens and pinks
Mixing together to make the perfect splash of
color

Off the Spring Prince goes to see the King
Whistling along to the canaries song
Happy as can be
Back from guarding the city
Ready to hear the news the King has to say
Off the Spring Prince goes to see the King

Summer Prince

The birds sing a tuneful song
To say that the day will be long
But a good day is about to begin

The summer skies sparkle and shine
Like a new-filled glass of white wine
And the trees stand taller
Looking more green than a sea-green colored
collar

No wind stirs, for the Summer Prince has come
Through the moss-green woods
He rides on his glowing white steed
All animals rise to gaze up at this handsome man
With blonde hair that shines like the Heavens
And plump red lips that looks like a blooming
rose
And eyes that sparkle like the starry night blue
skies

The Summer Prince rides his steed
Into the Palace of Vibranside
Where his King awaits
To see if he has news about the gates

Walking down the grand halls of lush green
Listening to the birds in full song
Blonde-haired bangs bobbing along with his
stride
The Summer Prince has never felt pride
He takes care of his people as well as the land
Ensuring that nothing can break through
To stop the peace and life that thrives
In the Summer Prince's home of Vibranside

Autumn Prince

Long burgundy hair flows down to his waist
Soft to the touch and flowing in the breeze
The thick Redwood trees rustle in the wind
As if bowing down to the Autumn Prince
Along he rides atop his steed

With the billowing robes that were cut
Professionally to fit his muscular frame
Colors of red and orange that splash together
In a vibrant wave of power for everyone to see
The Autumn Prince rides to see the King

The short drying grass is in no comparison
To his hazel-green specked eyes
As he rides through the forest where
The Season is in full bloom
The Autumn Prince carries a thin but powerful
sword at his side
As one of the protectors of the land of
Vibranside

He is serious when he needs to be
But when his Season is awaiting its turn
He likes to stay in his castle of Autumnseed

He is the signifying Season when the city is
guarded
By himself and the change in the year
He signifies a new life from such a long breath

Where the birds aren't out as long
And the people of Autumn begin to play
While the Autumn Prince guards them
But now he rides to see the King
In hopes that things will be better
And the people can sing once again

King of the Seasons

As the King of the Seasons waits
Siting on his throne
Patiently waiting for the Princes of the Seasons
To tell them about news of the land

When the Princes arrive they bow down to the
King
Rising then, to meet his gaze while the birds
outside sing
The Princes of the Seasons try not to move
Under the powerful eyes of the King
"My sons" the King says, his voice soft yet deep
and stern
"I have called you all to counsel today on behalf
of some tremendous news."
The Princes nod in unison slowly
Trying not to grow more eager to see what their
King, their father, has to say

The King waits out his next sentence patiently,
gaging their reactions
And then he smiles cheerfully
"In honor of each of you for your bravery on
protecting this wonderful land,
I have set up a feast where

We can all take a stand.”
The Winter Prince clears his throat softly as he
Looks up at his King
"What's the catch, father? There must be
something
Else you're wanting to say."
The King of the Seasons smiles and bows his
head
Thinking thoughtfully of the Winter Prince
And his other sons
"As a reward for protecting our people, we
Have been brought news of a blessing. An elder
man has four daughters
Who are all wanting to marry.
I have accepted, wanting the best for my sons."
The Princes bowed, trying to contain their
excitement in front of their King.
Eager to meet these four women that this elderly
man offered to them
For protecting the lives and the land
They so graciously love

www.ingramcontent.com/pod-product-compliance
Lightning Source LLC
Chambersburg PA
CBHW070614160726
48003CB00005B/2267